D1143297

C333427820

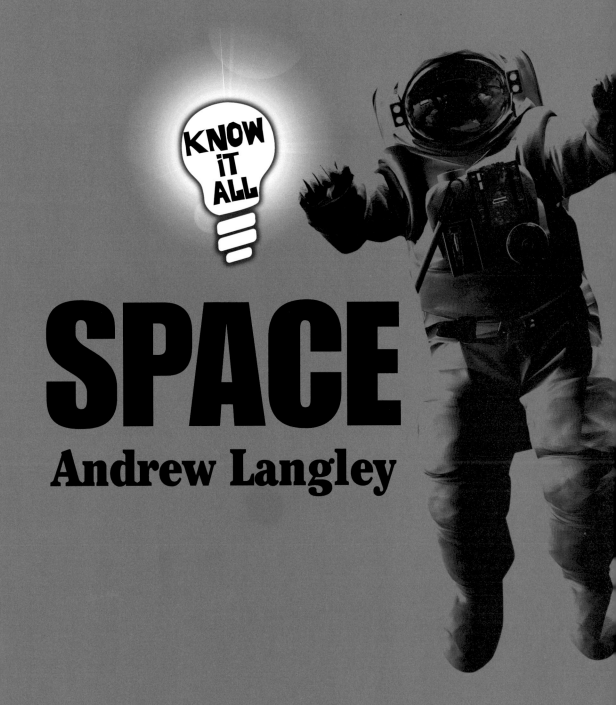

KNOW iT ALL

SPACE
Andrew Langley

W

FRANKLIN WATTS
LONDON • SYDNEY

First published in 2013
by Franklin Watts

Copyright © Franklin Watts 2013

Franklin Watts
338 Euston Road
London NW1 3BH

Franklin Watts Australia
Level 17/207 Kent Street
Sydney, NSW 2000

All rights reserved.

Series Editor: Amy Stephenson
Planning and production by Discovery Books Ltd
Editor: James Nixon
Series designer: D.R. ink
Picture researcher: James Nixon
Picture credits: cover image (NASA)
Alamy: p. 4 (Bruno Sinnah). Corbis: pp. 18 bottom (Jon Hicks), 29 top (Victor
Habbick Visions/Science Photo Library). NASA: pp. 5 bottom (M Weiss/CXC),
6 bottom (SDO/AIA), 8 top (JPL/USGS), 11 top and middle (JPL), 11 bottom (Voyager
2 Team), 12 top and bottom (JPL-Caltech), p13 top (JPL-Caltech), 14 (A Nota/ESA),
15 top (M Livio and the Hubble 20th Anniversary Team/ESA), 17 top (JPL-Caltech/
ESA/Harvard-Smithsonian), 17 bottom (M Robberto [Space Telescope Science
Institute/ESA] and the Hubble Space Telescope Orion Treasury Project Team,
20 top and bottom, 21, 22, 23 left and right, 24 (Craig Atteberry), 25 top, 25 bottom
(JPL-Caltech), 26 (CXC), 27 (JPL-Caltech), 28 (JPL-Caltech). Shutterstock: pp. 5 top
(Igor Zh), 6 top (iurii), 9 bottom (Triff), 10 (Oko Laa), 13 bottom (mozzyb), 15 bottom
(jupeart), 16 (Jack Ammit), 18 top (ella1977), 19 top (Neo Edmund), 19 bottom
(Manamana), 29 bottom (Julien Tromeur).

Every attempt has been made to clear copyright. Should there be any inadvertent
omission please apply to the publisher for rectification.

Dewey number 520
ISBN: 978 1 4451 1827 7
Library ebook ISBN: 978 1 4451 2542 8

Printed in China

Franklin Watts is a division of Hachette Children's Books,
an Hachette UK company.
www.hachette.co.uk

CONTENTS

All words in **bold** can be found in the glossary on page 31.

WHAT IS SPACE?

The Earth seems huge to us. Yet it is one small planet that **orbits** around a star – the Sun. On a clear night you can see thousands and thousands of other stars – many have their own planets orbiting them. The stars are surrounded by vast areas of nothingness, which we call space. In the never-ending stretches of space, our Earth is just a tiny speck.

AMAGING FACT
Light years

The stars are so far away that we measure the distance with a special unit, called a light year. A light year is the distance light travels in one year – nearly 10 trillion* km (6 trillion miles). The nearest star to Earth apart from the Sun is called Alpha Centauri, and it is over four light years away. Can you work out how many kilometres that is?

*1 trillion = 1 million x 1 million.

SPACE JOKE

Q What's a light year?

A The same as a regular year, but with fewer calories!

Our Earth is just one tiny planet in a gigantic universe.

BIG BANG

How did the universe begin? Scientists believe it started with a 'Big Bang', over 13 billion years ago. This bang released a vast amount of energy into what was then a very small universe. The energy blew the universe into bits, which eventually became stars, planets and other bodies in space. They are still flying apart, like a gigantic explosion that goes on and on.
As the stars keep moving away from each other the space between them – and the universe – grows bigger and bigger.

The universe started to grow when extremely hot, **dense matter** blew apart in a giant explosion we call the 'Big Bang'.

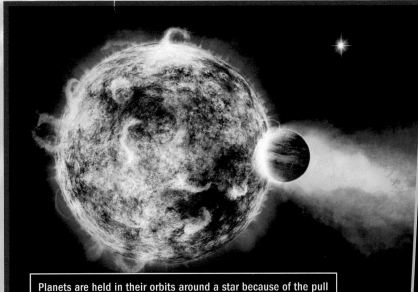

Planets are held in their orbits around a star because of the pull of the star's gravity. This planet is orbiting so close to its star that it is being destroyed by the star's powerful energy.

TRUE OR FALSE?

There is no **gravity** in space. True or False?

FALSE! Without gravity there would be no universe. Gravity is a force that can move everything in the universe, helps stars and planets form and keeps planets in their orbit around a star. The pull of gravity is stronger or weaker depending on how much **mass** an object has. The Earth has a greater mass than your body, so its pull of gravity stops you from floating away from the surface. The Earth has less mass than the Sun, which is why we orbit around it.

THE SUN

The Sun is our nearest star, but it is still more than 150 million km (90 million miles) away! It produces so much light and heat that part of this reaches us here on Earth. Without the energy **radiating** from the Sun, nothing on Earth could live. It would be a dark, dead planet.

The Sun is a million times bigger than the Earth. It is not rocky, like Earth, but a ball of glowing gas. About 70 per cent of this is **hydrogen**, and 28 per cent is **helium**. Under high **pressure** at the **core** of the Sun, these gases release huge amounts of energy in the form of light and heat. The Sun's core is very hot. The temperature inside can reach an amazing 15 million °C.

SUN JOKE

'Living on Earth is expensive – but it does include a free trip around the Sun every year!'

AMAZING FACT
Solar flares

Sometimes an extra-massive release of energy spurts from the Sun. This is called a solar flare. Flares erupt as far as 800,000 km (500,000 miles) out into space. They throw out clouds of **particles**. These can have serious effects for us on Earth because they damage radio communications with **satellites**. Worse still, the rays from flares are dangerous for **astronauts** working in space outside the protective shield of the Earth's **atmosphere**.

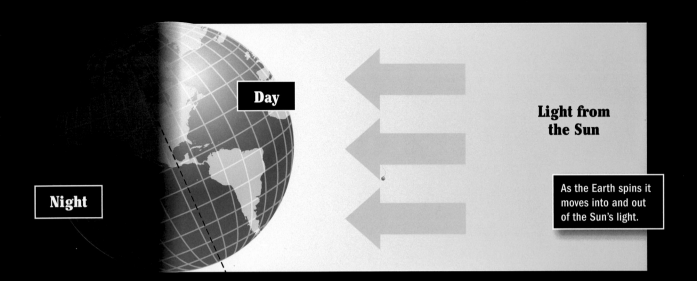

Day

Night

Light from the Sun

As the Earth spins it moves into and out of the Sun's light.

DAY AND NIGHT

The Earth takes one year to orbit the Sun. The Earth is also spinning as it orbits the Sun. As it spins, different areas of the planet move into the Sun's light. When our part of the Earth faces the Sun, we have day (above). When it faces away from the Sun, we have the darkness of night. Earth takes 24 hours (a day) to do one full spin. The Earth is tilted as it spins. During the year different parts of Earth are tilted towards the Sun (below). This gives us the seasons.

TRUE OR FALSE?

Light from the Sun takes more than 8 minutes to travel to Earth. **True or False?**

TRUE! In fact, the Sun's light reaches us in about 8 minutes and 20 seconds.

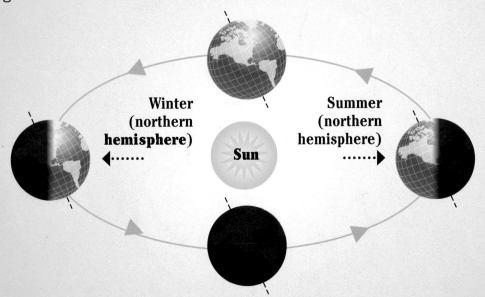

Winter (northern hemisphere)

Summer (northern hemisphere)

Sun

When your part of Earth is tilted towards the Sun, you have summer. When your part of Earth is tilted away from the Sun, you have winter.

THE MOON

The Moon looks very big and bright in the night sky. This is because it is so close – just 384,000 km (239,000 miles) away. In fact it is about 50 times smaller than Earth. The Moon is our nearest neighbour in space. It travels in orbit around the Earth. Six of the planets in the **solar system** have moons orbiting around them.

WHY DOES THE MOON SHINE?

When it is full, the Moon is the brightest object in the night sky. It makes no light of its own, but simply reflects the light from the Sun. So why does it seem to change shape from night to night, gradually waxing (getting bigger) or waning (getting smaller)?

The Moon makes one complete journey around the Earth every 27.3 days (almost one month). We see different amounts of the Moon's sunlit side depending upon where it is in the night sky.

AMAZING FACT
The dark side of the moon

During each trip around the Earth, the Moon **rotates** only once. This means that the same side is always facing us. We never get to see the other side of the Moon. In 1959 a Russian rocket travelled around the Moon and sent back photos of what we call its 'dark' side. But it is not always dark: the Sun shines on it for roughly two weeks every month.

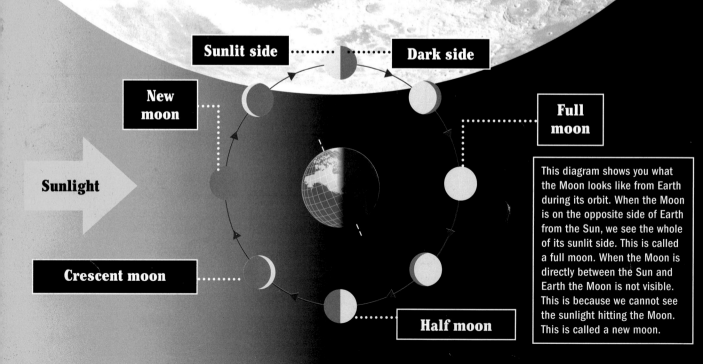

Sunlit side

Dark side

New moon

Full moon

Sunlight

Crescent moon

Half moon

This diagram shows you what the Moon looks like from Earth during its orbit. When the Moon is on the opposite side of Earth from the Sun, we see the whole of its sunlit side. This is called a full moon. When the Moon is directly between the Sun and Earth the Moon is not visible. This is because we cannot see the sunlight hitting the Moon. This is called a new moon.

BLOCKING OUT THE SUN

Amazingly, the Moon can cast a shadow on the Earth. Even though the Moon is tiny compared with the Sun, it is much nearer to us. Roughly once every two years, it passes directly between the Sun and part of the Earth. It blocks out the Sun's light for a few moments, causing darkness during the day. This is called a solar **eclipse** (below).

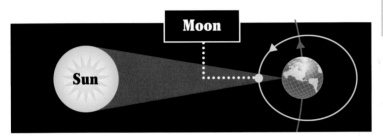

TRUE OR FALSE?

The Moon moves very slowly. It travels around the Earth at only 35 kph (20 mph). **True or False?**

FALSE! The Moon actually hurtles around the Earth at an average speed of about 3,700 kph (2,300 mph)!

SPACE JOKE

Q How does the man on the Moon cut his hair?

A Eclipse it!

THE MOON AND THE TIDES

The Moon is held in its orbit by the strong pull of Earth's gravity, which acts like a magnet. But the Moon also has its own gravity. This is much weaker than Earth's gravity, yet it is strong enough to pull large areas of water on Earth towards it. This causes sea levels to rise and fall, an effect we call the **tides**.

THE SOLAR SYSTEM

PLANET JOKE

Q Where do Martians go for a drink?

A To a Mars bar!

Earth is not the only planet circling the Sun. There are seven other major planets, as well as **dwarf planets**, moons, rocks, dust and gas clouds all swirling around our star. Together these make up the solar system. The pull of the Sun's gravity stops them shooting off into space.

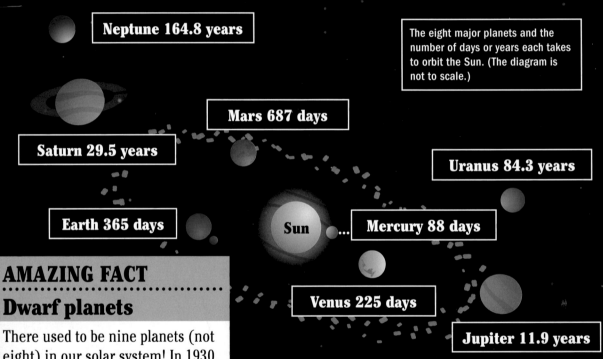

Neptune 164.8 years

The eight major planets and the number of days or years each takes to orbit the Sun. (The diagram is not to scale.)

Mars 687 days

Saturn 29.5 years

Uranus 84.3 years

Earth 365 days

Sun ... Mercury 88 days

Venus 225 days

Jupiter 11.9 years

AMAZING FACT
Dwarf planets

There used to be nine planets (not eight) in our solar system! In 1930, **astronomers** discovered a small, new planet, much further away than Neptune. They called this ninth planet Pluto. But recently scientists have discovered other similar-sized planets, such as Ceres and Eris, and think there are probably hundreds more. They decided that these smaller planets including Pluto should be called dwarf planets instead.

THE EIGHT MAJOR PLANETS

MERCURY is closest to the Sun. It has no atmosphere. The temperature can be as low as -170°C at night and as high as 420°C in the day!

Venus

VENUS would be impossible to live on. It is covered in clouds of poisonous gas and the atmosphere has a pressure 92 times stronger than on Earth. Venus is also the hottest planet, with temperatures reaching 460°C!

EARTH has two crucial ingredients for life – breathable air in the atmosphere and water. The atmosphere also blocks out some of the Sun's **rays**, which would otherwise be harmful to us.

MARS is called the 'Red Planet', because of the iron **deposits** that give the planet its red colour. Unmanned spacecraft have also found traces of frozen water here. Mars is very cold, with an average temperature about the same as winter at Earth's South Pole.

JUPITER is the largest planet in the solar system, ten times bigger than Earth. It is made mostly of gas and liquid, with a small core of rock. Jupiter's most dramatic feature is the Great Red Spot measuring about 32,000 km (20,000 miles) across. This is actually a permanent swirl of red storm clouds.

Jupiter

Great Red Spot

SATURN is another 'gas giant', like Jupiter. It is easy to recognise from the nine flat rings that spin around its **equator**. The rings are made up of fragments of rock and ice. Saturn has more than 60 moons, plus thousands of moonlets (small moons) fixed inside its rings.

URANUS is made mostly of ice and rock. Around it swirls a cloud of gases, which gives the planet a bluey-green colour. It is the coldest planet in the solar system with a recorded temperature of -224°C!

The dark spots on Neptune show the extreme storms that rage in its atmosphere.

TRUE OR FALSE?

Saturn is so light it would float on water. **True or False?**

TRUE! Saturn is a huge planet, but it is not very heavy. It is less dense than other planets – and water, so it would certainly float. The biggest difficulty would be finding a stretch of water big enough!

NEPTUNE is another 'ice giant', like Uranus. It is the furthest planet from the Sun. The wind speeds on Neptune can reach a staggering 2,100 kph (1,300 mph)!

A storm of comets fly near a rocky planet. One of the comets has struck the planet's surface.

COMETS AND ASTEROIDS

Have you ever seen a comet, with its long, brilliant tail? Or a shooting star? These are just two of the amazing things which come from far out in the solar system. Sometimes they travel near the Earth – and a few even fly straight into it!

DIRTY SNOWBALLS

A comet is like a gigantic dirty snowball flying through space. It is mostly a mass of frozen dust and gases. Around this is a fuzzy cloud of more gas and dust, called a coma. If a comet flies near the Sun, its heat melts some of the ice. This forms a shining tail that streams out for millions of kilometres behind the comet.

There are thousands of comets on their long orbits around the Sun. Most are not bright enough to see, but a few shine brilliantly as they pass near the Earth. The most famous is Halley's Comet. Named after the astronomer who discovered it, the comet appears roughly every 75 years. This was last seen in 1986 – so look out for its next appearance in 2061!

Many stars are orbited by a ring of asteroids called an asteroid belt.

ASTEROIDS

An asteroid is a lump of rock and metal that orbits the Sun. There are millions of these objects, usually less than 1.6 km (1 mile) across. Most of them are trapped between Mars and Jupiter, and are held there by Jupiter's gravity. This is known as the 'asteroid belt'.

MEET THE METEORS

What is a shooting star? It is not a star at all, but a small chunk of rock called a meteoroid, chipped off when asteroids smashed into each other. Some meteoroids fly into Earth's atmosphere, reaching enormous speeds. The friction (rubbing) of the air heats them until they glow, leaving a bright trail in the sky. This is what we call a shooting star, though the correct name is a meteor.

Most meteors burn up before they hit the Earth. But some pieces survive to reach the surface. These are called meteorites. Scientists believe as much as 10,000 tonnes of meteoroid material falls on our planet every day. In 2013 a meteor measuring 20 metres across exploded in the sky over Russia. The energy from the blast shattered the windows of buildings, injuring 1,500 people.

Large asteroids in the asteroid belt can smash into each other, which can send pieces of them flying towards Earth.

AMAZING FACT
The biggest meteorite

Two billion years ago a monster meteorite smashed into the Earth in what is now South Africa. It was at least 10 km (6 miles) wide and created a **crater** which was 300 km (180 miles) in diameter. Called the Vredefort Crater, it is probably Earth's biggest ever meteorite impact.

SPACE JOKE

Q Where does an astronaut park his spaceship?

A At a parking meteor!

STARS

How far away are the stars (not counting the Sun)? If you got into the fastest spacecraft ever built, and flew in a straight line for about 80,000 years, you might reach the nearest star. And if you kept going for another billion years, you might reach the most distant stars.

Stars do not shine forever. They are always changing very slowly, in a cycle that takes billions of years. The cycle begins when they form and ends when they die. During this cycle they change in size, temperature and colour.

AMAZING FACT
How many stars are there?

Nobody knows the exact total number of stars – and probably nobody ever will. But scientists believe there are at least 10 sextillion of them. That's 10^{21}, or 10,000,000,000,000,000,000,000!

TRUE OR FALSE?

Stars twinkle. **True or False?**

FALSE! All stars give out a steady supply of light. But we do not see this. The stars' rays have to pass through the Earth's atmosphere to reach us. The moving layers of air and moisture in the atmosphere bend and twist the rays – and so the starlight appears to twinkle.

Younger stars are blue in colour. Older stars appear redder.

HOW STARS ARE FORMED...

A star begins as a dark cloud of **cosmic** dust and gas (mainly hydrogen). The force of gravity at the centre sucks in the cloud, creating huge amounts of pressure and heat. The hydrogen changes into helium, and the energy produced creates light. A new star is born.

New stars are born in towers of gas like these.

When big stars die they blow apart in a massive explosion called a supernova.

...AND HOW THEY DIE

After about 10 billion years, the supply of hydrogen starts to run out. The star produces less energy and cools down, growing redder in colour. At the same time the star **expands**, ending up as a large, cool star called a red giant. Very big stars die much more quickly. They simply blow themselves apart in a gigantic explosion, known as a supernova (left). The eighth brightest star in our sky, Betelgeuse, is dying and could explode in a supernova soon – or it might not be for thousands of years. When this does happen, scientists think that people on Earth will see Betelgeuse outshining the Moon for about three months!

Our galaxy, called the Milky Way, can be seen in the night sky as a long, fuzzy band.

GALAXIES

Look up at the sky on a clear summer night with no Moon. You may be able to see a thick, hazy, glowing band stretching across from one horizon to another. This is the Milky Way. Our solar system, with the Sun at its centre, is part of this gigantic band, which contains more than 100,000 million stars.

The Milky Way is just one of the many **galaxies** in space. It is shaped in a flat spiral, with curved arms that spin around the central point. Our Sun is just a tiny dot near the edge of one of these arms. But, if we are part of a spiral, why does the Milky Way look like a straight band? The answer is that we are looking sideways from inside the galaxy, and so we see a flat edge.

TRUE OR FALSE?

The word 'galaxy' means 'milky. **True or False?**

··

TRUE! 'Galaxy' comes from the Greek word 'galaxias', which means 'milky'. It refers to the faint, milky appearance of our own galaxy when seen from Earth.

AMANZING FACT
AMAZING FACT
How many galaxies are there?

The number of galaxies in space is mind-boggling. Astronomers calculate that there are at least 170 billion of them. Some have spiral shapes, while others are elliptical (lozenge-shaped) or star-shaped.

This spiral-shaped galaxy known as Messier 81 is 12 million light years away from Earth and one of the brightest galaxies that can be seen through a telescope.

CLOUDY SHAPES

A galaxy contains more than stars. Inside it are the fragments of dead stars, and big clouds of dust and gas. These are called nebulae (from the Latin word 'nebula', meaning a cloud). Some are dark, like the Horsehead Nebula. Others are light, like the Orion Nebula, which you can see as a fuzzy glow in the sky.

These pillars of dust and gas make up the Orion Nebula. Over 1,300 light years away, it is the closest place to Earth where new stars are forming.

LOOKING AT THE STARS

When you first look at the night sky, it seems a jumble of stars. But in time you can learn to recognise patterns. Long ago people gave names to the star patterns they saw. They called them after animals (like the Great Bear) or gods (like Orion). These patterns are called **constellations**.

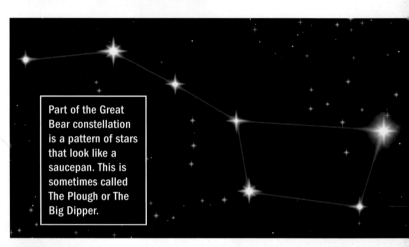

Part of the Great Bear constellation is a pattern of stars that look like a saucepan. This is sometimes called The Plough or The Big Dipper.

This astronomer is using a computer to help him find stars through his telescope.

SEEING FURTHER

People used to believe the Earth was the centre of the universe, and that the stars and planets moved around it. The invention of the telescope in the early 1600s made it possible for astronomers to see things in the sky that no one had ever seen before, such as the rings on Saturn. Gradually, people discovered how massive and complex the universe was, and how small and insignificant the Earth was.

Today, astronomers use huge telescopes to study the universe. Some have curved lenses or mirrors which gather and **magnify** light from space to form images. These are called optical telescopes, which are used for looking closely at the planets.

SIGNALS FROM SPACE

Optical telescopes are not powerful enough to examine the stars because the stars are too far away. Instead astronomers use radio telescopes to collect **radio waves**. These have huge curved dishes that focus the radio waves and turn them into electric signals. Powerful computers can turn these signals into images.

Radio telescopes point to the sky at the Very Large Array observatory in New Mexico, USA.

AMAZING FACT
Telescope in space

The Hubble Space Telescope was launched in 1990, and has been in orbit around the Earth ever since. This satellite can 'see' much further and more clearly than any other telescope. The images sent back by Hubble have helped astronomers to answer many questions, such as: 'How old is the universe?' (over 13 billion years). Hubble is due to be replaced in 2018 by the James Webb Space Telescope.

SPACE JOKE

Q What kind of light goes right around the Earth?

A A satellite!

SPACE TRAVEL

Imagine you are strapped in a tiny **capsule** on top of a giant rocket, 100 metres high. The rocket shudders as its engines thunder into life. They blast you up from the launch pad. Within minutes you are hurtling away from Earth and out of the atmosphere. Soon you are travelling through the blackness of space!

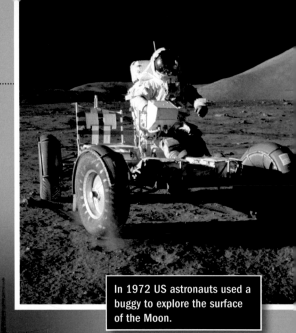

In 1972 US astronauts used a buggy to explore the surface of the Moon.

THE FIRST PERSON IN SPACE

The very first rocket to go into space was launched by the Germans during World War II in 1942. It simply went up and came down again. In 1957, the Russians put the first satellite, called *Sputnik*, into orbit around Earth. In 1961, the Russians also put the first human in space, a pilot, Yuri Gagarin.

LANDING ON THE MOON

In July 1969 the first humans landed on the Moon. US spacecraft *Apollo 11* flew through space for nearly three days before going into orbit around the Moon. *Apollo 11* had two parts. One astronaut, Michael Collins, orbited the Moon on board the Command Module while two others landed on the surface in the Lunar Module (landing craft).

AMAZING FACT
Escaping gravity

The *Apollo* spacecraft that took humans to the Moon was carried out into space by powerful *Saturn V* rockets. These rocket engines were strong enough to overcome the pull of Earth's gravity. Taller than the Statue of Liberty, they weighed as much as 400 elephants. Their engines produced over 3,400 tonnes of **thrust** at take-off.

A *Saturn V* rocket launches *Apollo 11* into space in 1969.

No one knew what the Moon's surface would be like. Luckily, it was firm enough for the Lunar Module to land safely. The two astronauts, Neil Armstrong and Buzz Aldrin, stepped out onto the Moon. After collecting rock samples and setting up scientific equipment, they took off again and rejoined Collins. *Apollo 11* headed back to Earth.

THE SPACE SHUTTLE

American astronauts made five more landings on the Moon. The last was in 1972. Since then, American manned space flights have used a craft called the space shuttle. This looks like an ordinary aircraft. It is carried into space by a rocket, and then orbits on its own before returning to Earth and landing on a runway.

Space shuttles were used for many projects, including building and maintaining the Hubble Space Telescope. The final shuttle mission was in 2011, although a new spacecraft is being developed to replace them.

TRUE OR FALSE?

The first animal to go into space was a monkey. **True or False?**

FALSE! The first living creatures in space were fruit flies, sent up in a US rocket in 1947. The first four-legged space traveller was a Russian dog called Laika, who died during the flight. There is a memorial statue of Laika (standing on top of a rocket), at the launch site near Moscow.

SPACE JOKE

Q Where do astronauts keep their sandwiches?

A In their launch boxes!

The *Atlantis* space shuttle touches down on the runway after a 14-day mission in space.

LIVING IN SPACE

The first astronauts only stayed in space for a few days. Since then, people have lived in space stations for much longer. A Russian, Valeri Polyakov, stayed in space for a record 438 days in 1994–1995. Living in space can be extremely dangerous.

INSIDE A SPACECRAFT

Some problems astronauts face are obvious. Space travellers have to take all their food, which is usually tinned or dried. They have to breathe the same air time after time, **filtering** it to remove harmful gases. They also have to recycle water, collecting and cleaning every drop – from water vapour breathed out to urine from the toilets. Even laboratory rats' urine is reused!

Much more dangerous are the effects of weightlessness. Because astronauts can't feel the effect of gravity in their spacecraft, everything is weightless. Astronauts' bodies do not have to work very hard, so muscles, heart and blood vessels become weak. Blood and other fluids move up to the head, causing puffiness, sickness and headaches. Astronauts exercise regularly to keep themselves healthy.

AMAZING FACT
Life back on Earth

A long stay in space causes astronauts problems when they return home. One surprising effect is that space travellers are so used to objects floating weightless that they frequently drop things on the floor!

An astronaut in space is strapped to a running machine so he can get the exercise he needs without floating away.

EXIT

WHY WEAR A SPACESUIT?

Outside of the spacecraft space is a deadly place for humans. There is no oxygen to breathe. The lack of **air pressure** would make your blood and body fluids boil. There are the dangers of being hit by a meteoroid, or harmed by **radiation** from the Sun. An astronaut always wears a spacesuit outside the spacecraft. This protects the wearer from rays and flying objects. There are also tanks that provide oxygen to breathe.

An astronaut goes on a space walk in their spacesuit to carry out repairs to the outside of the International Space Station.

SCIENTISTS IN SPACE

The International Space Station (ISS) [above] is a research laboratory in space. Developed by the USA, Russia, Japan, Europe and Canada, it is home for a crew of up to six astronauts, who conduct scientific experiments. The ISS is made of several pieces which were launched separately, starting in 1998, and assembled in space.

INTO DEEP SPACE

It only takes three days to get to the Moon. But the journey to Jupiter takes three years, while Uranus is at least five years away. No human could make such a long journey out – and back again. So scientists use robot spacecraft called probes to explore and gather information about deep space beyond the Moon.

The main job of a space probe is to collect scientific information about the planets and the area of space it is passing through. Probes either fly past planets or land on their surfaces, then send back data and images to Earth. Many of these have given us our first close-up view of other planets.

TRUE OR FALSE?

In 2001, the Americans sent a probe to the Sun. **True or False?**

TRUE! The spacecraft *Genesis* could not go all the way to the Sun, of course, or it would have burned up. But it did fly towards the Sun and scoop up samples of **solar wind**. This is the mixture of gas and particles flowing away out of the Sun at up to 450 km (300 miles) per second. Scientists believed that these samples would help them understand what stars are made of. *Genesis* crash-landed back on Earth in 2004, but some samples survived and are still being analysed.

In 2004 the *Cassini-Huygens* probe was sent to explore Saturn and its moons. This artist's impression shows the *Huygens* probe nearing the surface of a moon called Titan while the *Cassini* spacecraft flies overhead.

In 2015 the *New Horizons* spacecraft, shown in this artist's impression, will give us the first ever close-up view of the dwarf planet Pluto.

EXPLORING THE PLANETS

Since the 1960s, space probes have travelled deeper and deeper into the solar system. A Russian probe crashed on Venus in 1967, and two US craft landed on Mars in 1976. In 1986, the European craft *Giotto* flew near Halley's Comet, to send back images and measurements. It even survived being hit by meteoroids! By 1989 probes had reached the most distant planets, Uranus and Neptune. Since 1997, probes have landed a number of mobile robots on Mars to analyse the surface.

In 2006 the *New Horizons* spacecraft was launched from the USA. Travelling at about 36,000 mph (58,000 kph) – faster than any previous human-made object – it reached the orbit of Uranus in 2011. *New Horizons* is expected to fly past the dwarf planet Pluto in 2015.

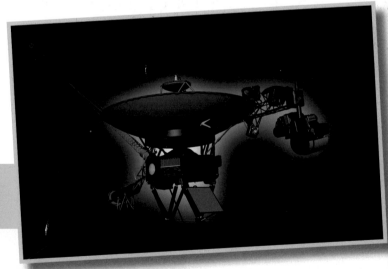

AMAZING FACT
Beyond the solar system

Which probe has gone the farthest? The answer is the American *Voyager 1* (right). Launched way back in 1977, *Voyager 1* has been flying away from Earth ever since! It has covered 11 billion miles (16 billion km), and sent back superb images of Jupiter and Saturn. In 2012, *Voyager 1* became the first spacecraft to leave the solar system and head for the distant stars. It is expected to continue sending signals back to Earth until around 2025.

BLACK HOLES AND QUASARS

The pull of a large star's gravity is very powerful, holding planets in its orbit. But what if a big star was squashed into a tiny ball? Its gravity would become far stronger – so strong that it would suck in everything nearby. Nothing could escape, not even rays of light. It would be a black hole in space.

Black holes certainly exist. They are created when a really big star is about to explode in a supernova at the end of its life. The central part of the star collapses into a small, but amazingly heavy core. It sucks in not just light, but any stars, gas and other space objects passing close by.

TRUE OR FALSE?

The Earth will be sucked into a black hole. **True or False?**

FALSE! Black holes do not go around eating up stars and planets. And there is no black hole near enough to the solar system to do that. Nor will the Sun eventually turn into a black hole – it is not a big enough star.

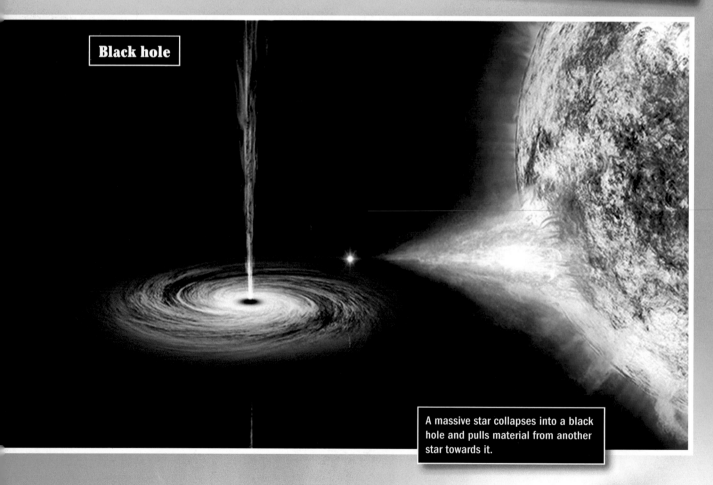

Black hole

A massive star collapses into a black hole and pulls material from another star towards it.

BRIGHTER THAN THE STARS

The largest black holes are called 'supermassives'. These probably lie at the centre of some galaxies in far distant space. What happens around supermassive black holes? The matter that is being sucked in from stars and space creates an enormous disc. As it swirls towards the black hole, the friction in the disc creates an enormous amount of energy and light – more than any other space body.

The result may be a quasar, short for 'quasi-stellar (star-like) radio source'. Quasars are the brightest objects in space – maybe a thousand times brighter than an ordinary galaxy. They are also the most distant objects ever discovered. The light from them has taken 10 billion years to reach us!

AMAZING FACT
How big is a black hole?

Black holes can be very big or very small. Scientists believe that the smallest black hole could be the size of a single **atom**! Yet inside this microscopic space could be crammed the 'mass' (amount of matter) contained in a huge mountain. The largest black holes have the mass of a million stars crushed together.

SPACE JOKE

Q What do you call an alien with three eyes?

A An aliiien!

Material is sucked into an enormous quasar, the brightest type of object in space.

THE FUTURE IN SPACE

Space is a hostile place. The danger of sudden death and disaster are always near. What's more, space exploration costs a staggering amount of money. Is it worth it? Many people think that space may be crucial to Earth's future – not just by showing us how the universe works and what it contains, but also as a source of important materials. We may even need to find a new home in space one day!

BACK TO THE MOON

The last person walked on the Moon over 40 years ago and it is not certain who will be next, but the Moon is about to get crowded. China plans to land two robot craft on the Moon to explore the surface. Russia is also sending a series of robot moon-landers, which will have sensors to examine what lies deep under the surface. Meanwhile, India will launch another robot explorer to collect rock samples. Space tourism could be the next big thing. A US company called Space Adventures is set to take two tourists on a flight around the Moon in 2015. One of the tickets has already been sold for 150 million dollars!

ROBOTS IN SPACE

We are already using robots instead of humans to explore planets. In the future, advanced robots will be sent to more distant and dangerous places in space. They may be landed on asteroids to collect rock samples. If humans decide to set up stations on the Moon or Mars, robots could be sent ahead to construct buildings and other equipment. These robots could be controlled by astronauts orbiting in space stations above.

Robots were recently sent to explore Mars. This robot is examining the rocks on Mars with a set of tools at the end of its arm.

NEW SPACECRAFT

As more stations in space and on other planets are built, new craft will be needed to shuttle astronauts to and from Earth. Some will be small, like the British 'Spacecab', which holds six people. Others, like the Japanese *Kankoh-Maru*, may carry up to 50 passengers. In the far future, unmanned craft may have sails, like ships. The idea is that these sails could be driven along by solar winds.

TRUE OR FALSE?

The Sun will last for another 4,000 years. **True or False?**

FALSE! The Sun will probably keep going for at least 4 billion years. But when stars eventually run out of energy they expand, cool and die. Life will no longer be possible on Earth without the Sun, so humans will have to find a planet in another solar system to live on. Maybe we should start looking now!

This artist's impression shows what a spacecraft of the future may look like with huge sails to drive it along.

AMAZING FACT
Is there anyone else out there?

As far as we know, life only exists on Earth. But somewhere in one of the billions of other galaxies something else may be alive. How do we find out? Recent findings on Mars have shown possible evidence of life forms, including frozen water and fossils of worms. Further **expeditions** will continue the search. Scientists also study cosmic dust, to see if it contains any signs of life and hunt for radio signals that could reveal the conversations of intelligent aliens!

QUIZ

How much have you learned about space from reading this book?
Here is a quiz to test your memory.

1. What is the name of the nearest star to Earth (apart from the Sun)?

2. What is the Moon doing when it is waxing?

3. What is the difference between a meteoroid and a meteorite?

4. Which galaxy is the Earth part of?

5. What was the name of the space probe which passed out of the solar system in 2012?

6. Which gas makes up most of the Sun?

7. What is a supernova?

8. Which planet is furthest away from the Sun?

9. How far is one light year?

10. In which year did people first land on the Moon?

11. What is the common name for a 'quasi-stellar radio source'?

12. What effect does the Moon have on Earth's oceans?

13. Between which two planets is the asteroid belt?

14. In which year will Halley's Comet reappear?

15. Which two planets are known as the 'gas giants'?

AMAGING FACT

How far from Earth?

The Moon	385,000 km (240,000 miles)
Venus (at its nearest)	38 million km (24 million miles)
The Sun	150 million km (95 million miles)
Asteroid belt	217 million km (135 million miles)
Neptune (at its nearest)	4,300 million km (2,700 million miles)
Alpha Centauri	44 trillion km (27 trillion miles)
Andromeda (the nearest galaxy to the Milky Way)	25 million trillion km (15 million trillion miles)

GLOSSARY

air pressure the force (pressure) applied in all directions by the air

astronaut a person who travels into outer space

astronomer someone who studies the universe

atmosphere the layer of gases which surround the Earth

atom one of the tiny particles which make up all matter

capsule a small spacecraft that contains the crew and is designed to be returned to Earth

constellation a group of stars

core the centre of something

cosmic belonging to the cosmos (universe)

crater a large hole or dent in the Earth's surface made by a falling object

dense thick, or crowded together

deposit material that is left behind

dwarf planet a planet that is orbiting the Sun which is not big enough to be classed as a major planet

eclipse when one object in space is blocked from view by another

equator the imaginary line around the surface of a planet which divides the northern hemisphere from the southern hemisphere

expand to grow larger

expedition a journey taken by a group of people with a definite aim

filter remove part of a liquid or gas as it passes through

galaxy a system of millions of stars held together by gravity

gravity the force which pulls objects together

helium a light and colourless gas found on Earth and in stars

hemisphere half of the Earth, usually divided into the northern and southern halves

hydrogen a colourless gas found naturally in the atmosphere and in space

magnify make something appear larger than it is

mass the amount of matter an object contains

matter everything which exists in the universe

orbit the path of a body travelling round another one

particle a very small piece of matter

pressure the force applied to a surface by something in contact with it

radiating giving out rays of energy

radiation waves of energy

radio waves waves in the air which carry electronic signals

ray a narrow beam of light

rotate spin round

satellite a spacecraft or other object which circles around something bigger

solar system the Sun together with the planets, asteroids and other objects in orbit around it

solar wind the flow of particles from the Sun travelling through space

thrust the force of a rocket engine which pushes a craft forwards suddenly

tide the rise and fall of the Earth's oceans, caused by the pull of the Moon

WANT TO KNOW MORE?

Here are some places where you can find out a lot more about space:

WEBSITES

http://www.aerospaceguide.net/space_kids.html
All kinds of information on space for homework and projects.

http://www.esa.int/esaKIDSen/LifeinSpace.html
The European Space Agency's website for kids.

http://www.kidsastronomy.com/
A beginner's guide to astronomy.

http://www.spacekids.co.uk/learn/
General space fun and information.

http://www.nasa.gov
The home of America's space agency.

BOOKS

Science FAQs: Why Are Black Holes Black? Questions and Answers About Outer Space, Thomas Canavan, (Franklin Watts 2013)

Space, Black Holes and Stuff, Glenn Murphy, (Macmillan 2010)

Space Travel Guides series, Giles Sparrow, (Franklin Watts 2013)

The Real Scientist: Space! Our Solar System and Beyond, Peter Riley, (Franklin Watts 2012)

The World in Infographics: Space, Jon Richards and Ed Simkins, (Wayland 2013)

Website disclaimer:
Note to parents and teachers: Every effort has been made by the Publishers to ensure that these websites are suitable for children, that they are of the highest educational value, and that they contain no inappropriate or offensive material. However, because of the nature of the Internet, it is impossible to guarantee that the contents of these sites will not be altered. We strongly advise that Internet access is supervised by a responsible adult.

INDEX